My name is
My birthday is on
My school is called
My teacher's name is
AF584371

Trace each letter when you have completed the matching pages in your work book. Draw something beginning with that letter in the frame.

Draw downstrokes to complete the pictures.

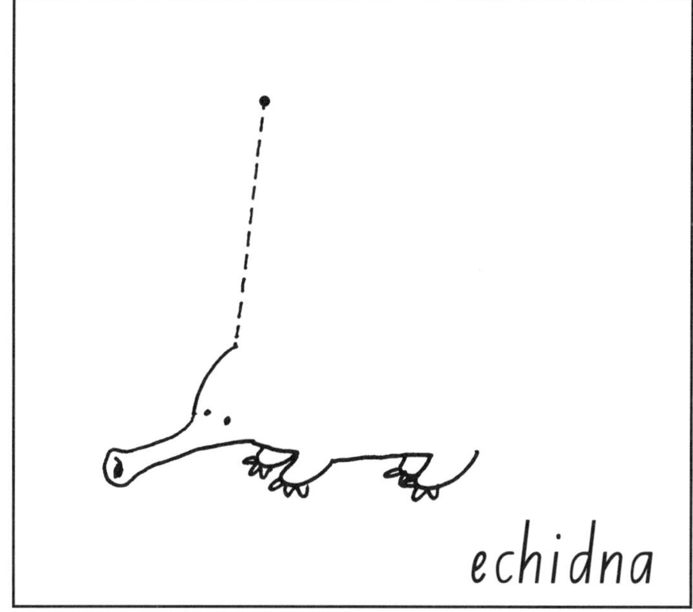

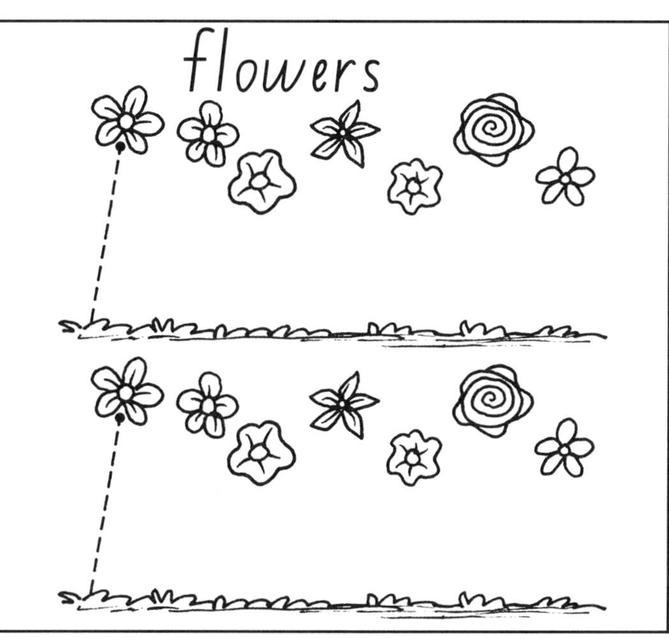

Underline all the downstroke letters in the sentence.

✓ your best l.

Downstroke pattern

The she f is fu of books.

Trace the head and body letters.

l t i f j x l z l j i t l

e_even 11 twe_ve 12

Trace. Copy. Draw.

shell skull

well doll

bell gull

Will Bill tell Nell?

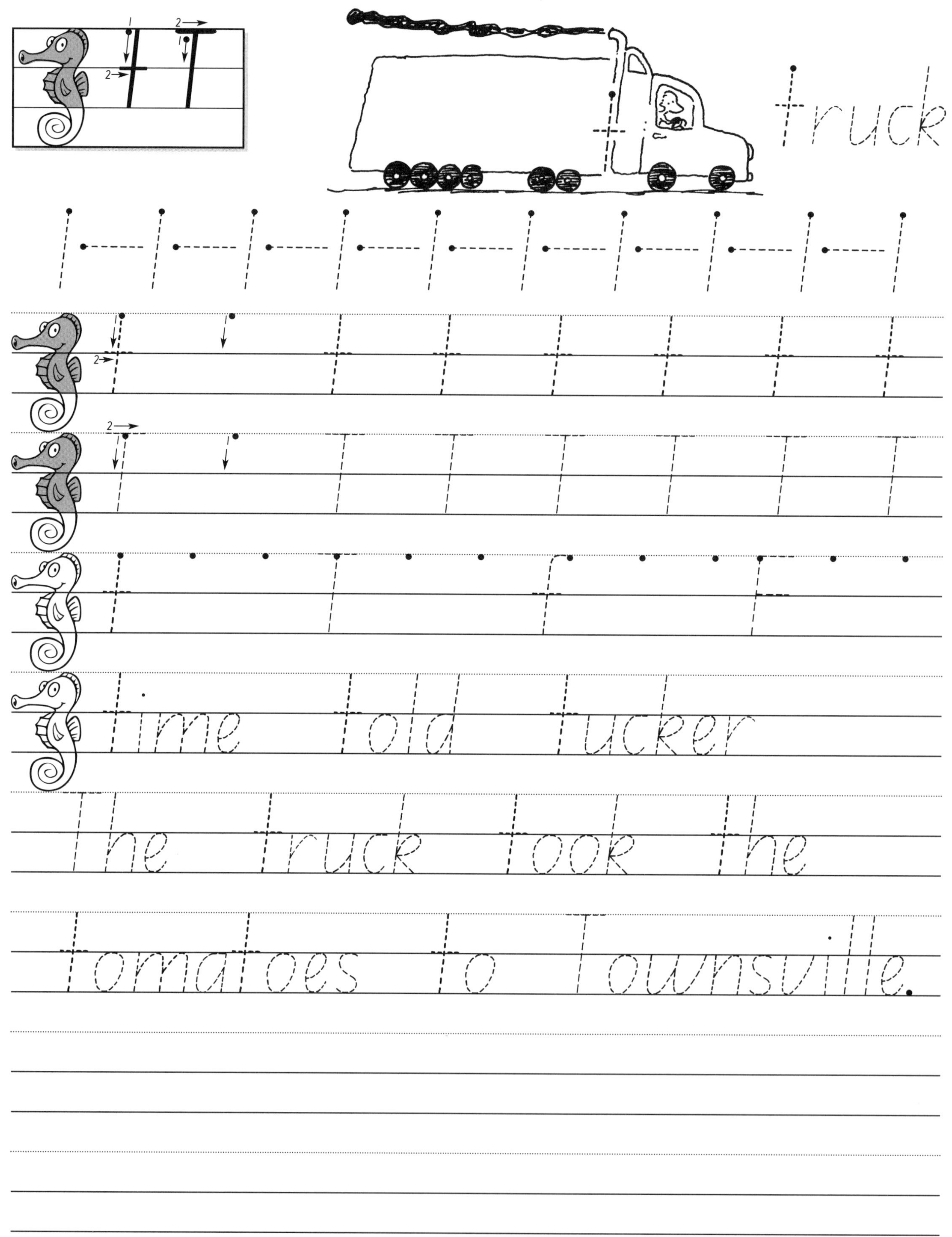

Underline all the head and body letters in the sentence.

Circle your best t.

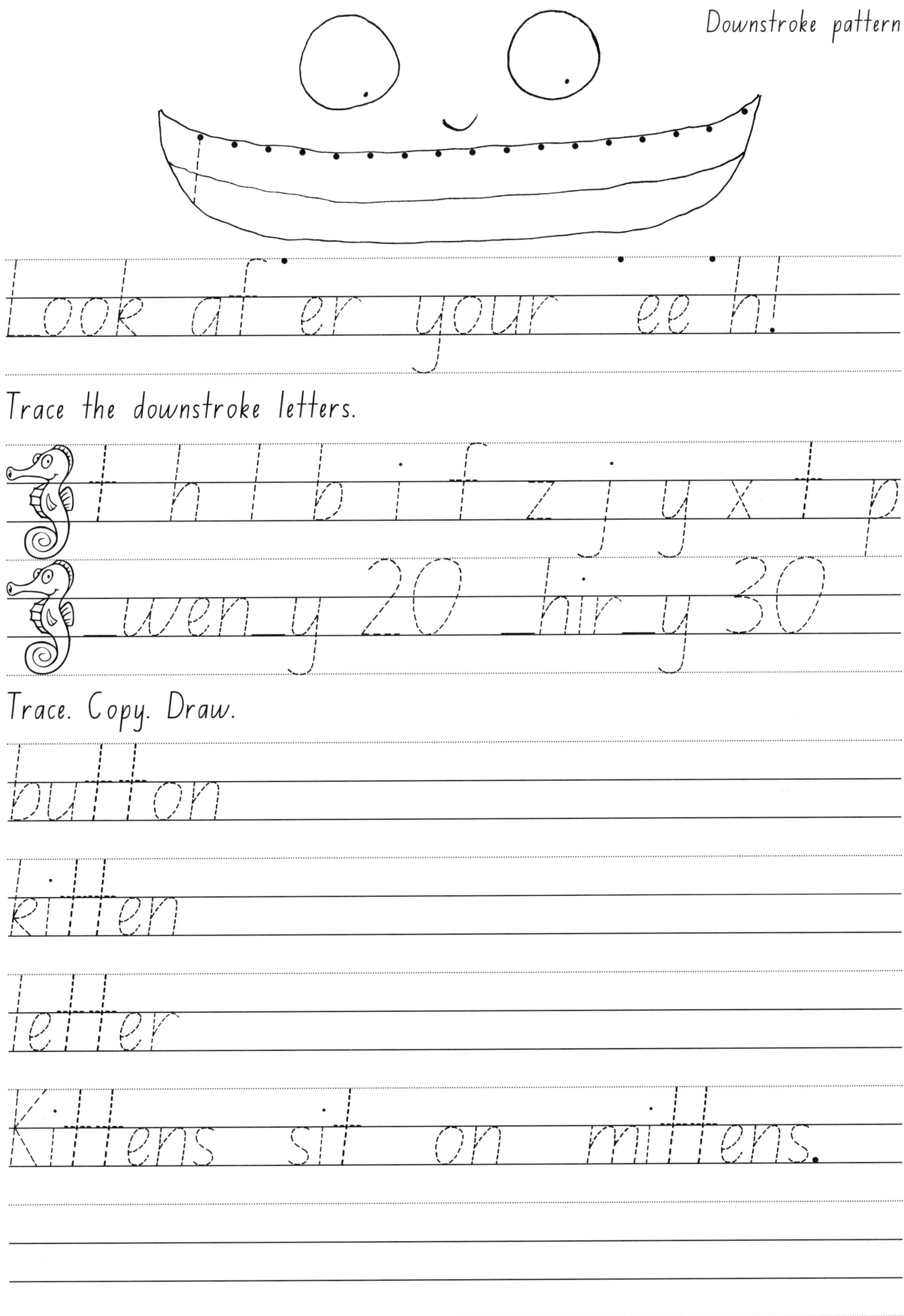

Look af er your ee h!

Trace the downstroke letters.

t h l b i f z j y x t p

_wen_y 20 _hir_y 30

Trace. Copy. Draw.

button

kitten

letter

Kittens sit on mittens.

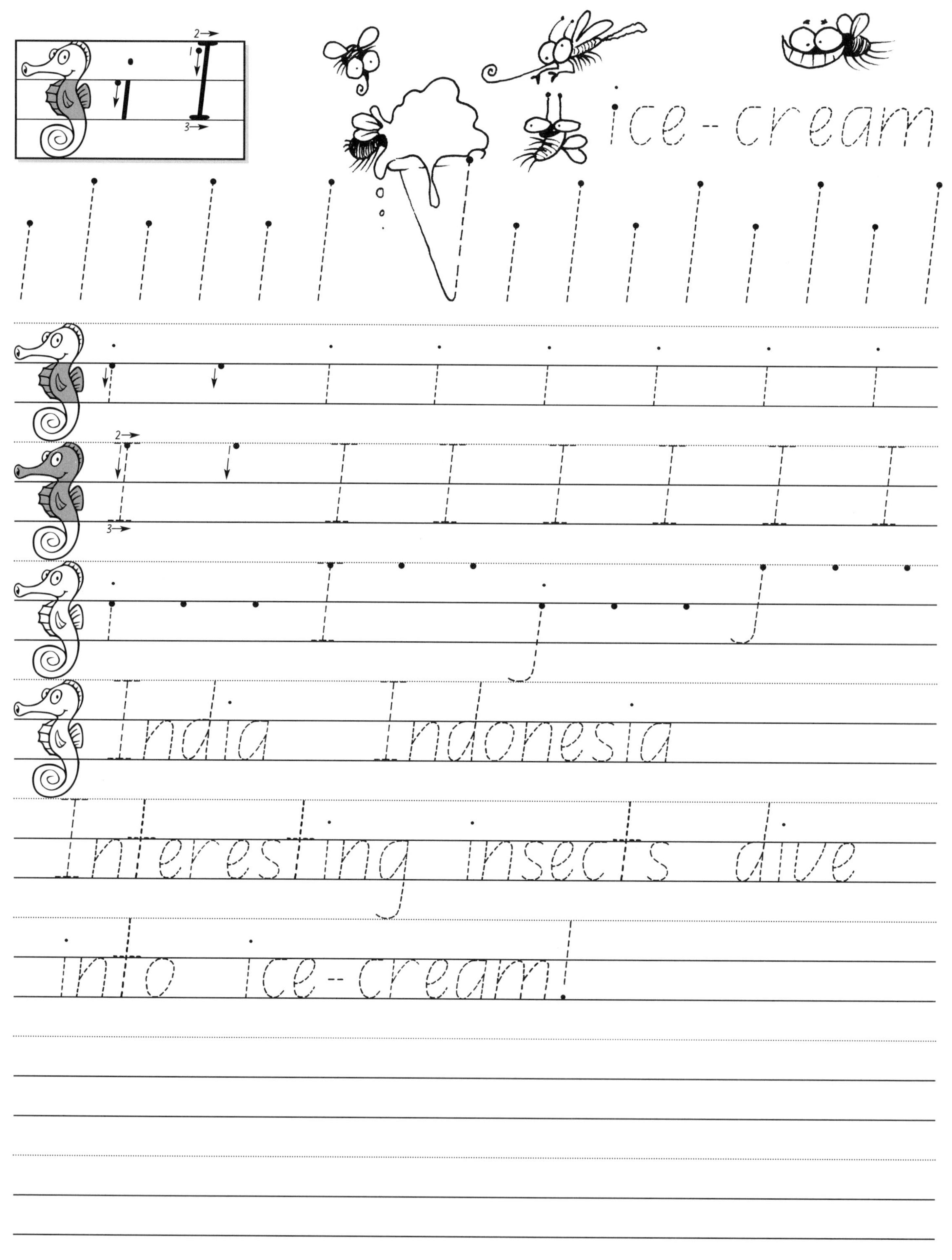

✓ all the downstroke letters in the sentence.

Circle your best i.

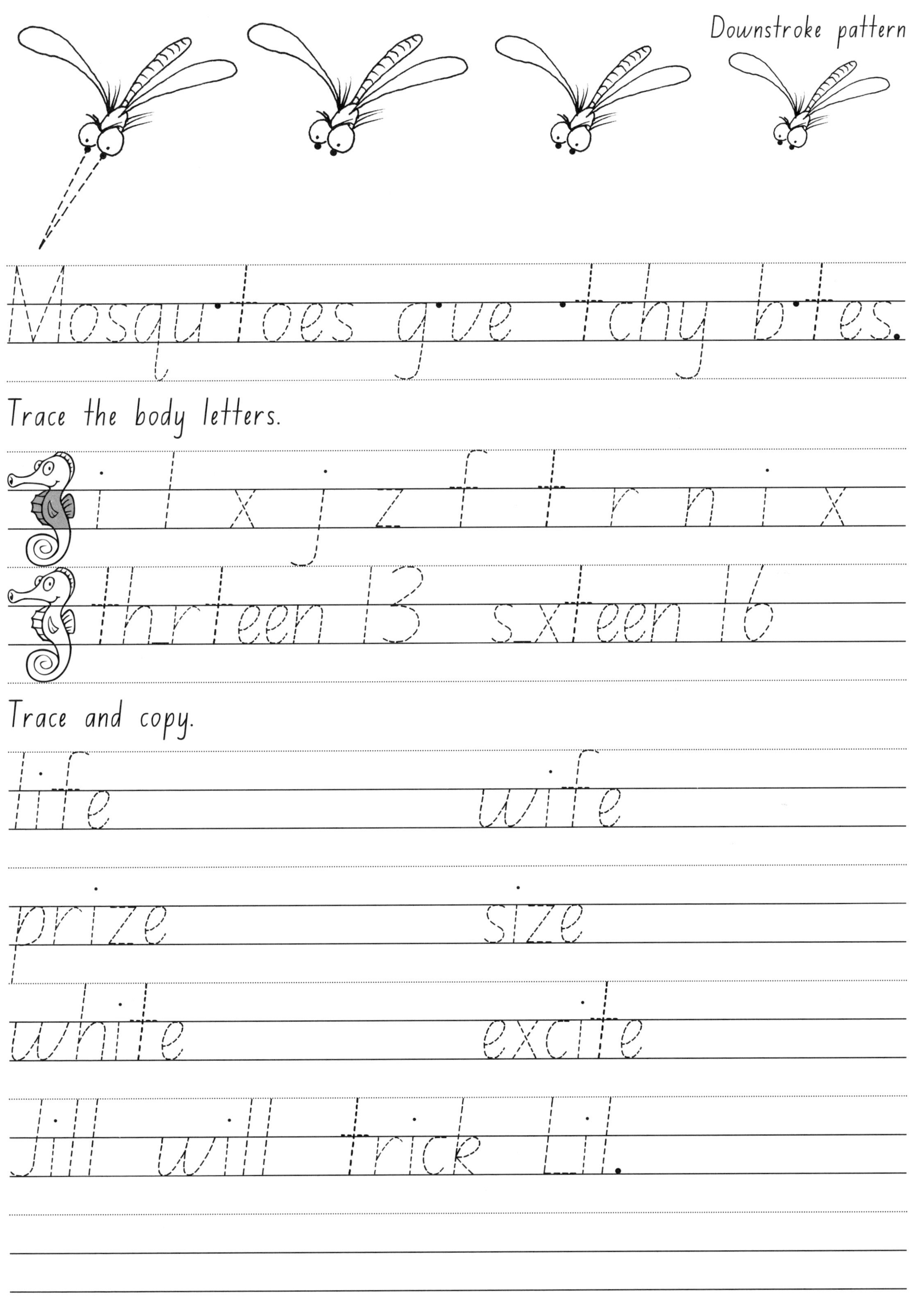
Downstroke pattern
Mosquitoes give itchy bites.
Trace the body letters.
i l x j z f t r n i x
thirteen 13 sixteen 16
Trace and copy.
life wife
prize size
white excite
Jill will trick Lil.

Re-trace the x's in the sentence in texta. Circle your best x.

Downstroke pattern

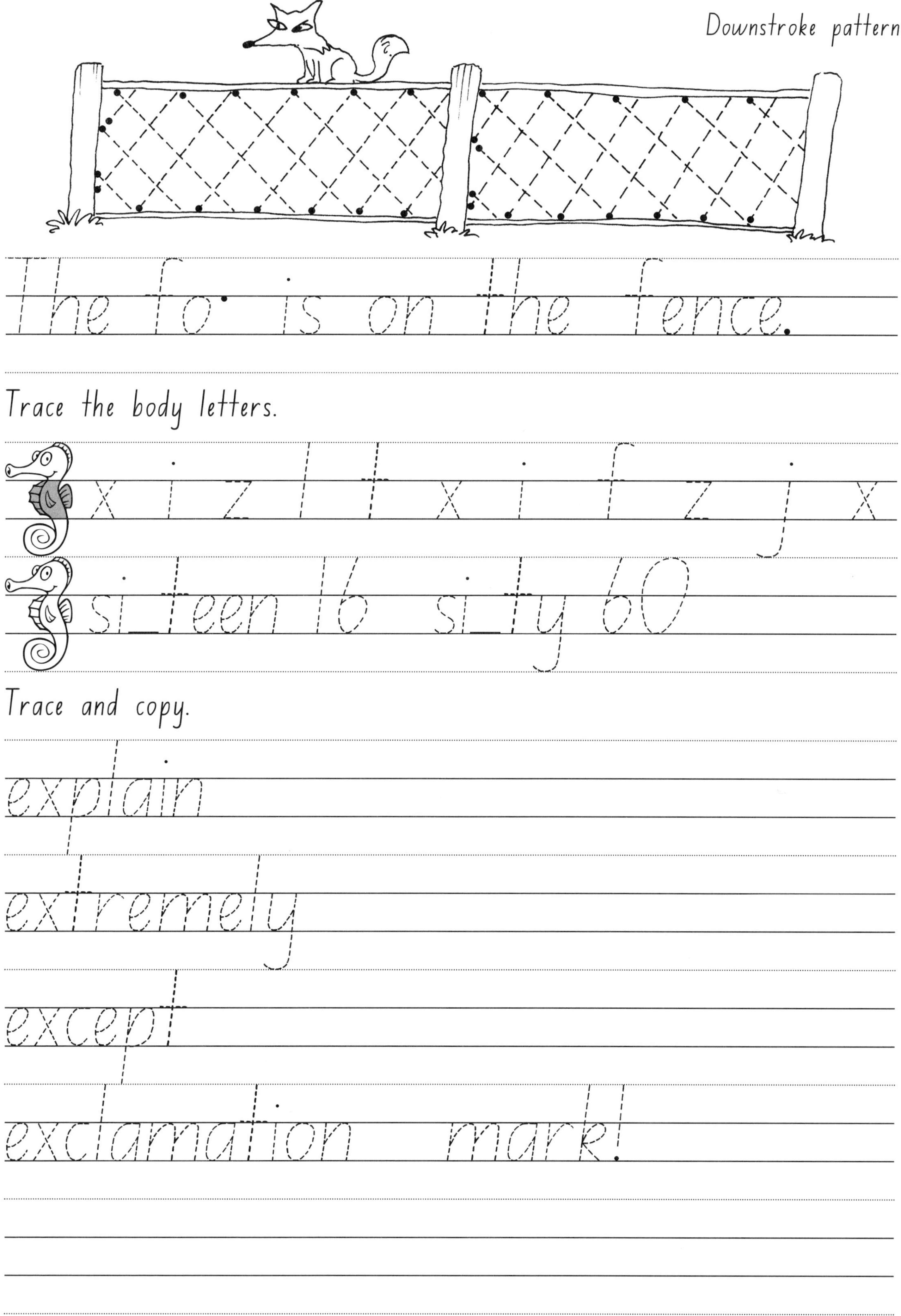

The fo· is on the fence.

Trace the body letters.

x i z l t x i f z j x

si_teen 16 si_ty 60

Trace and copy.

explain

extremely

except

exclamation mark!

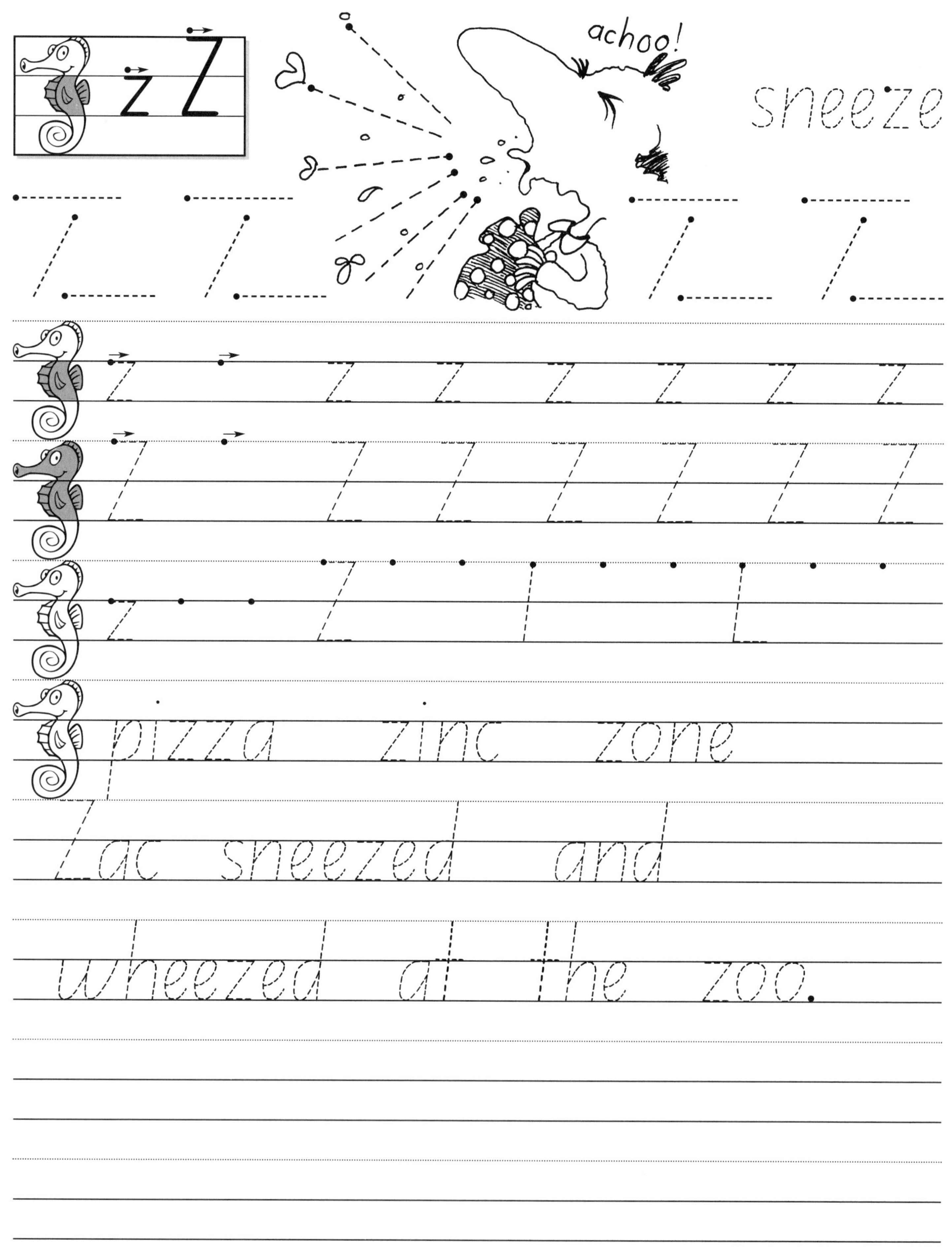

Look at the sentence. Re-trace the downstroke letters in red.

✓ your best z.

Downstroke pattern

I like pi__a best!

Trace these tricky letters.

z z z s s s z s z s z s

_ero 0 sub-_ero

Trace. Fill in the missing z's. Copy.

ja__ ma_e

ha_y do_e

la_y shoo_e

A zoological garden is often called a !

Put a wavy line under the downstroke letters in the sentence.

✓ your best f.

ive rogs ell.

Trace the head and body letters.

f t r i l h F x T f j b

_i_teen 15 _i_ty 50

Trace and copy.

traffic

different

sniff diff

Draw five soft toffees.

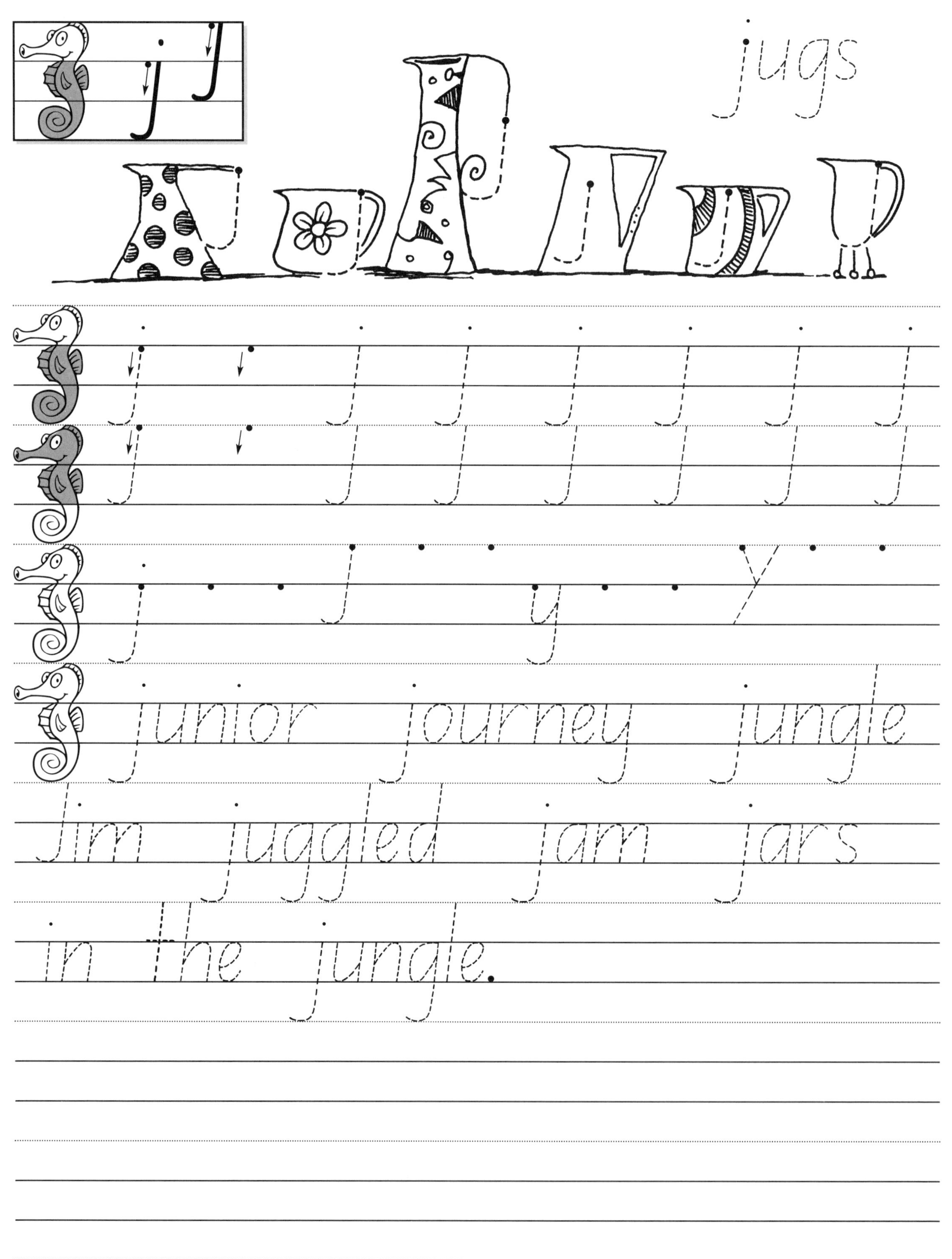

✓the downstroke letters in the sentence. Re-trace your best j in green.

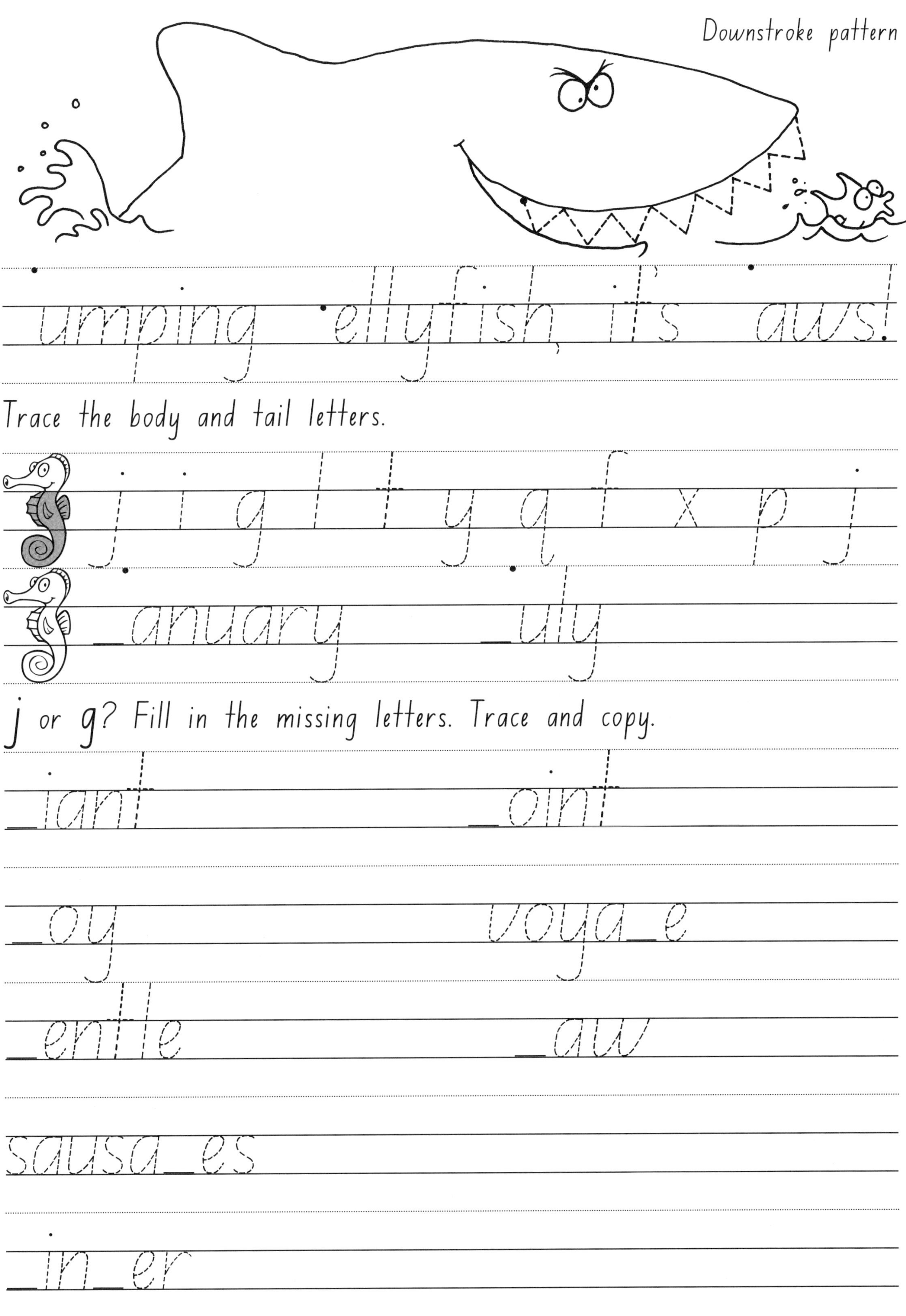

_umping _ellyfish, it's _aws!

Trace the body and tail letters.

j i g l t y q f x p j

_anuary _uly

j or g? Fill in the missing letters. Trace and copy.

_iant _oint

_oy voya_e

_entle _aw

sausa_es

_in_er

Trace. Copy. Write the matching capital letter.

l t f

i j x z

Trace and copy.

little exit

fizz jazz

fifty lift

Mark the starting point in red. Trace, then copy.

Colour the seahorse to show where the letters sit in the lines.

l t f

i x z

Draw the seahorse. Write all the downstroke letters.

Trace the hopping patterns to complete the pictures.

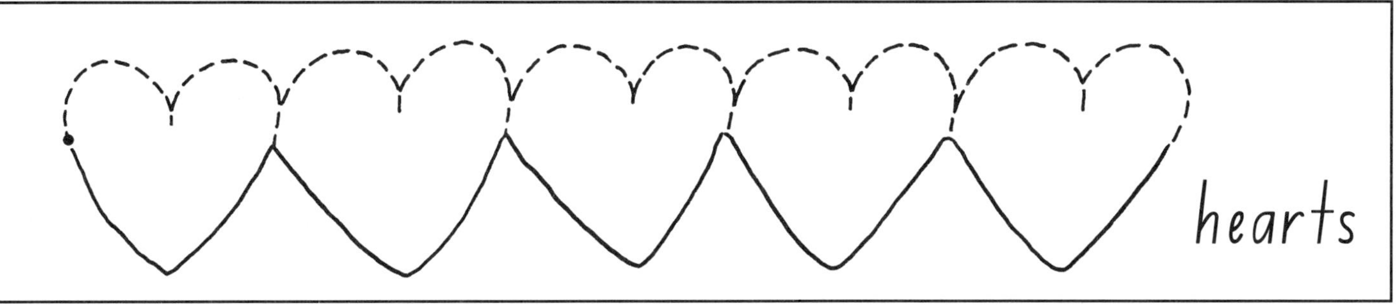

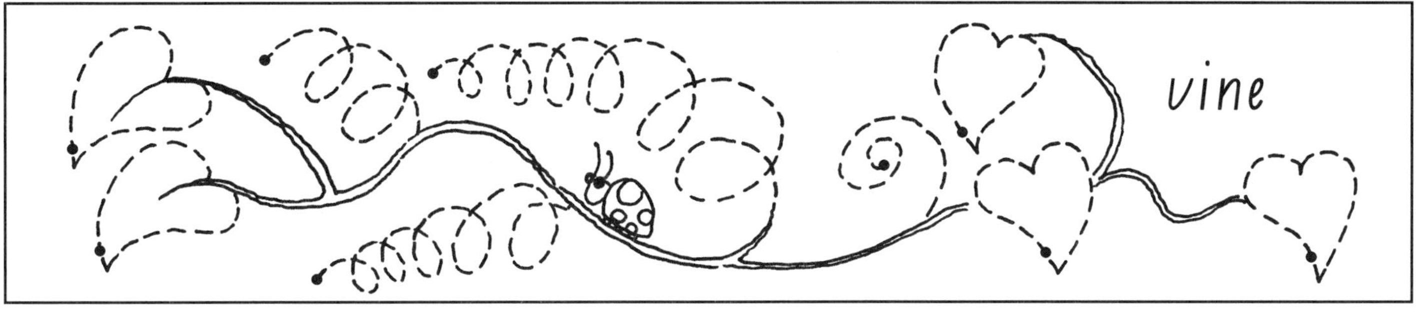

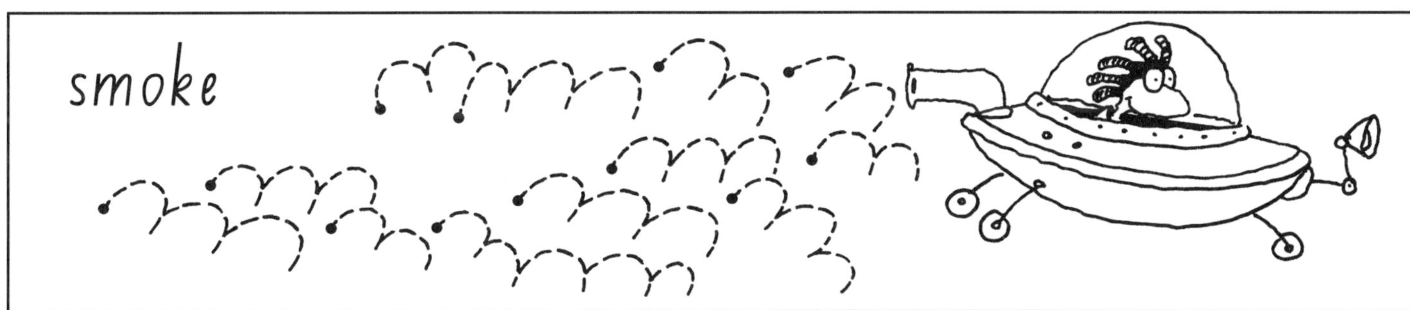

grandpa

Circle the hopping pattern letters in the sentence.

✓ your best m.

. . . , yu . , yu . !

Trace and colour the wedges, then copy.

m n r m

. arch . ay onth

Trace. Fill in the missing **m**'s. Copy.

__ushroo__s

pu__pkin

cru__pets

__uffins

__elon

Re-trace all the **n**'s in the sentence in blue. Underline your best **n**.

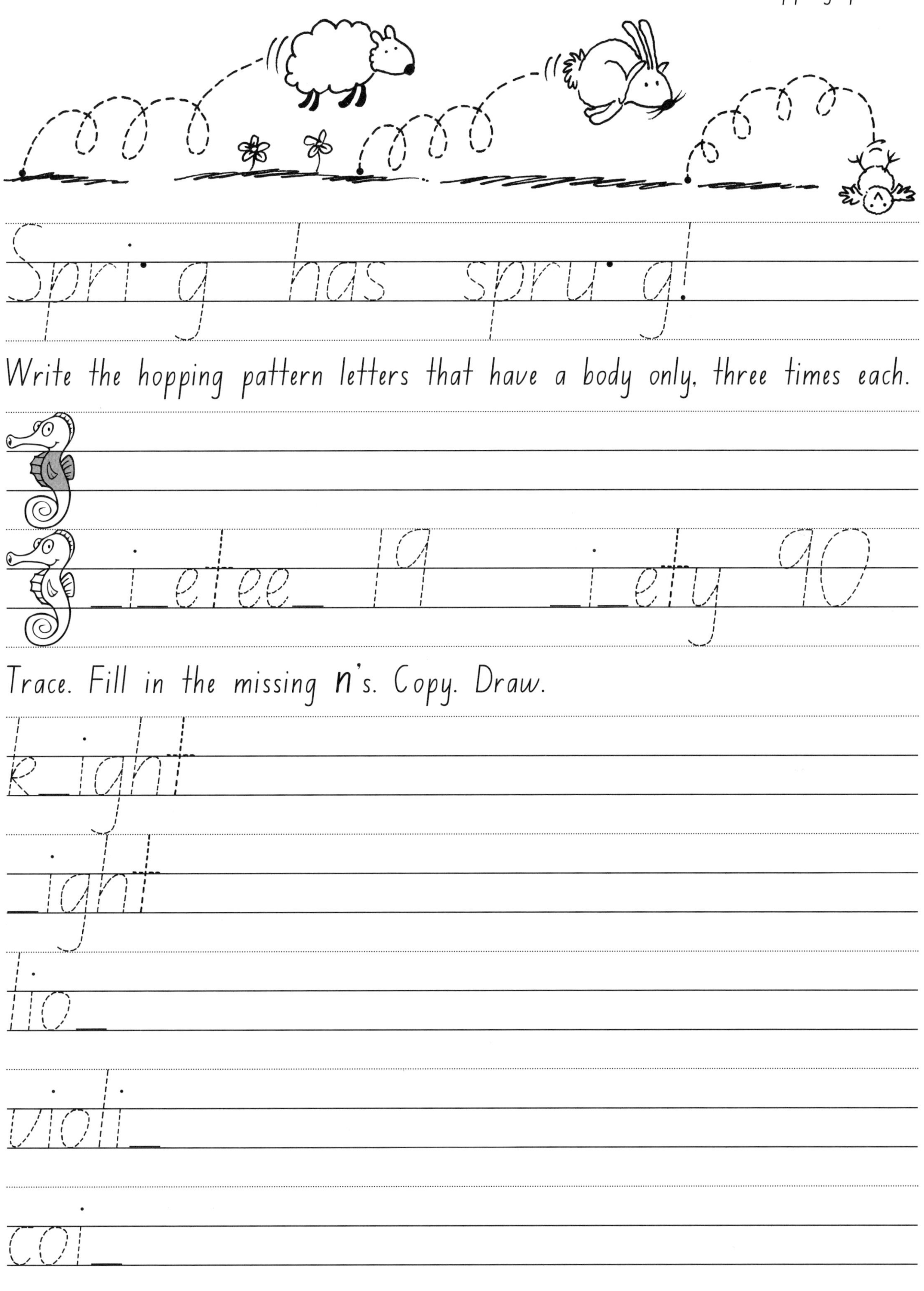

Spri g has spru g!

Write the hopping pattern letters that have a body only, three times each.

_i_etee_ 19 _i_ety 90

Trace. Fill in the missing **n**'s. Copy. Draw.

k_ight

_ight

lio_

violi_

coi_

Look at the sentence. Colour the wedges in the hopping pattern letters.
Circle your best **r**.

3 3 3 3 3 3 3 3 3

Colou every third 3 ed.

Find r in these letters.

n m p h k b n p

winte summe

Trace. Copy. Underline these letter patterns: **ar er ir or ur**.

hard star

verb her

girl first

born sport

turn purse

Underline all the hopping pattern letters in the sentence.

✓ your best h.

ere are some orses oes.

Write some head and body letters.

t irteen 13 t irty 30

Trace. Add letters to make new words.

has has_ _

her her_

heat heat_ _ heat_ _ _

her he_r he_r_

hop hop_ hop_f_ _

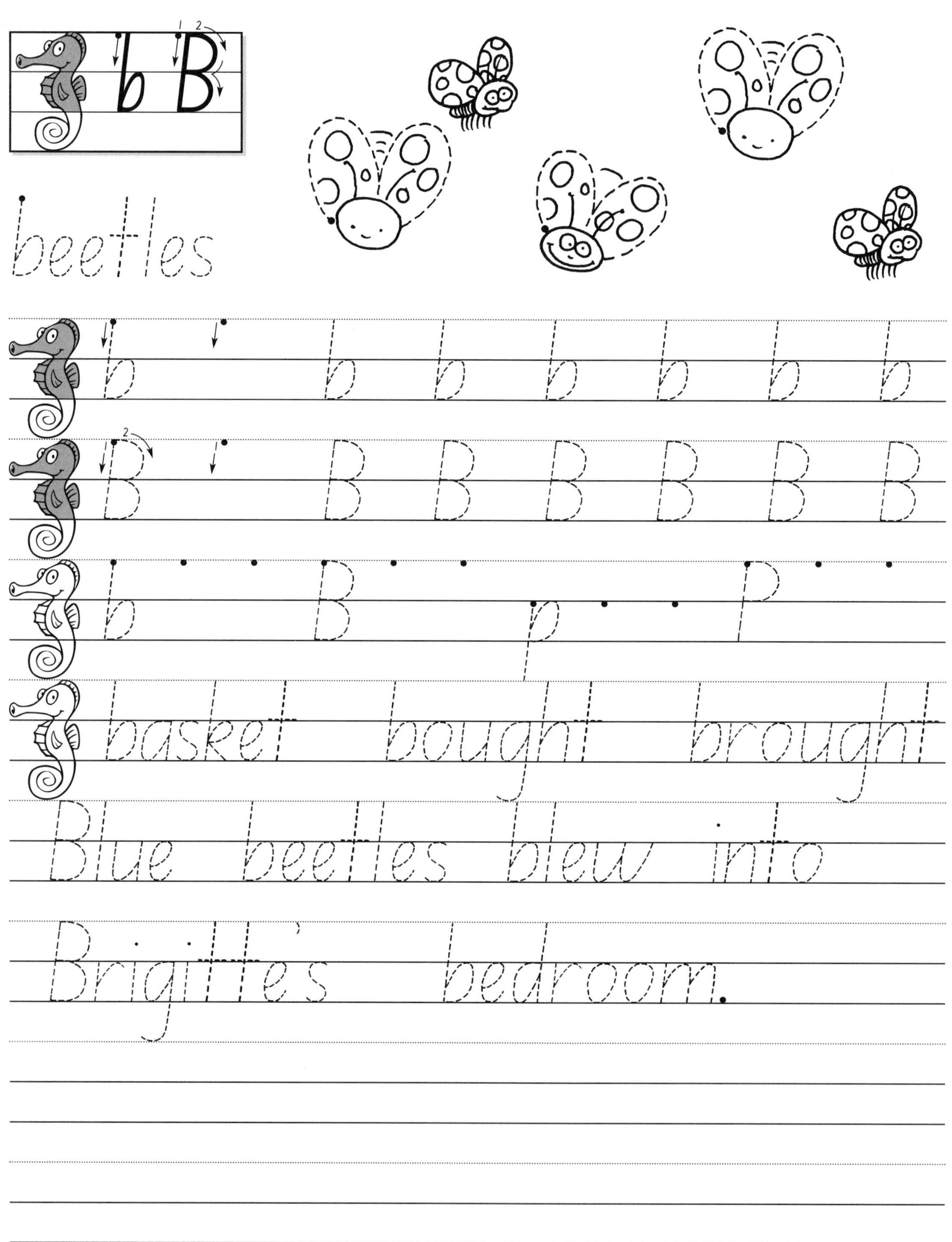

Re-trace all the b's in the sentence in blue. Underline your best b.

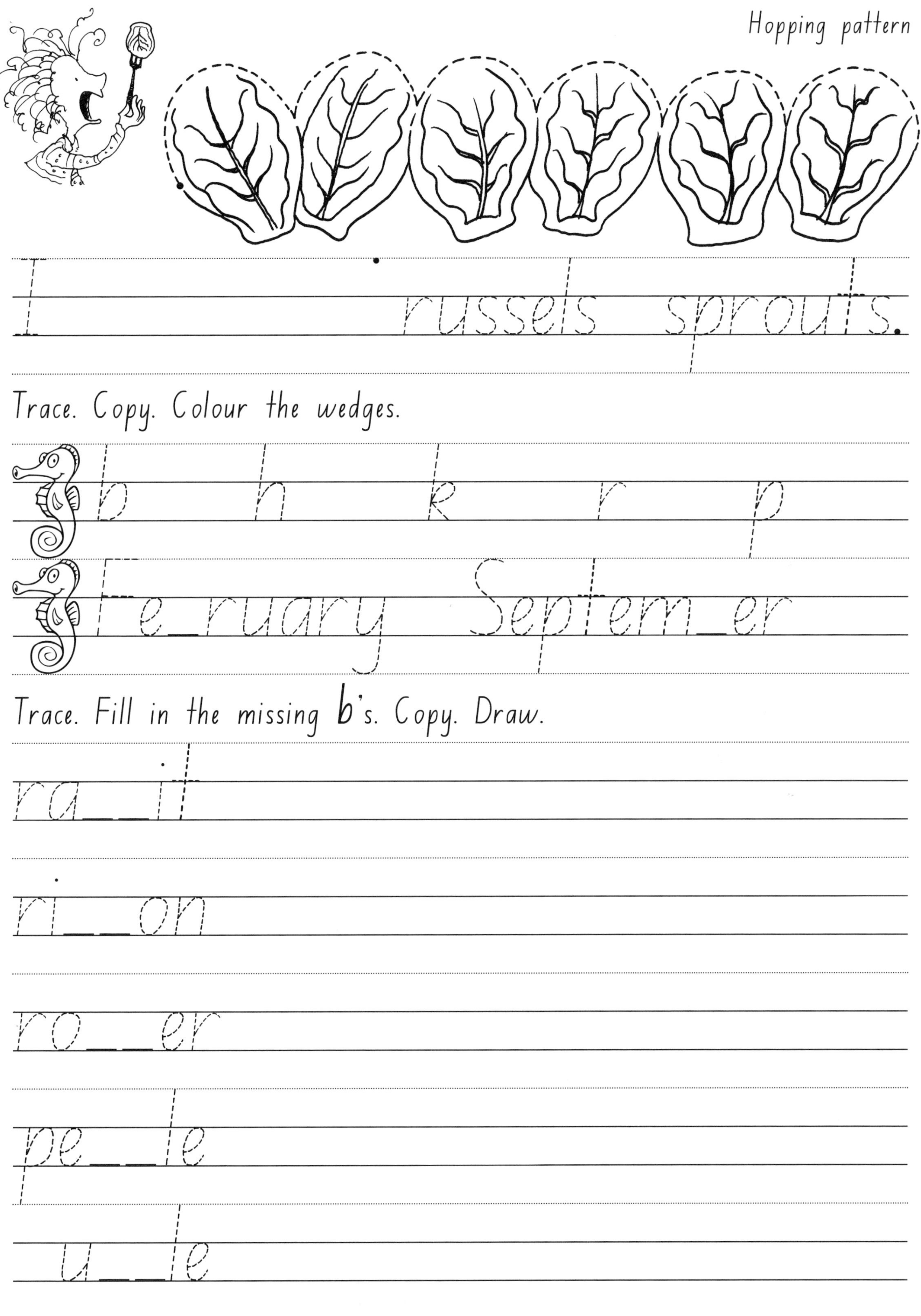

Trace. Copy. Colour the wedges.

Trace. Fill in the missing b's. Copy. Draw.

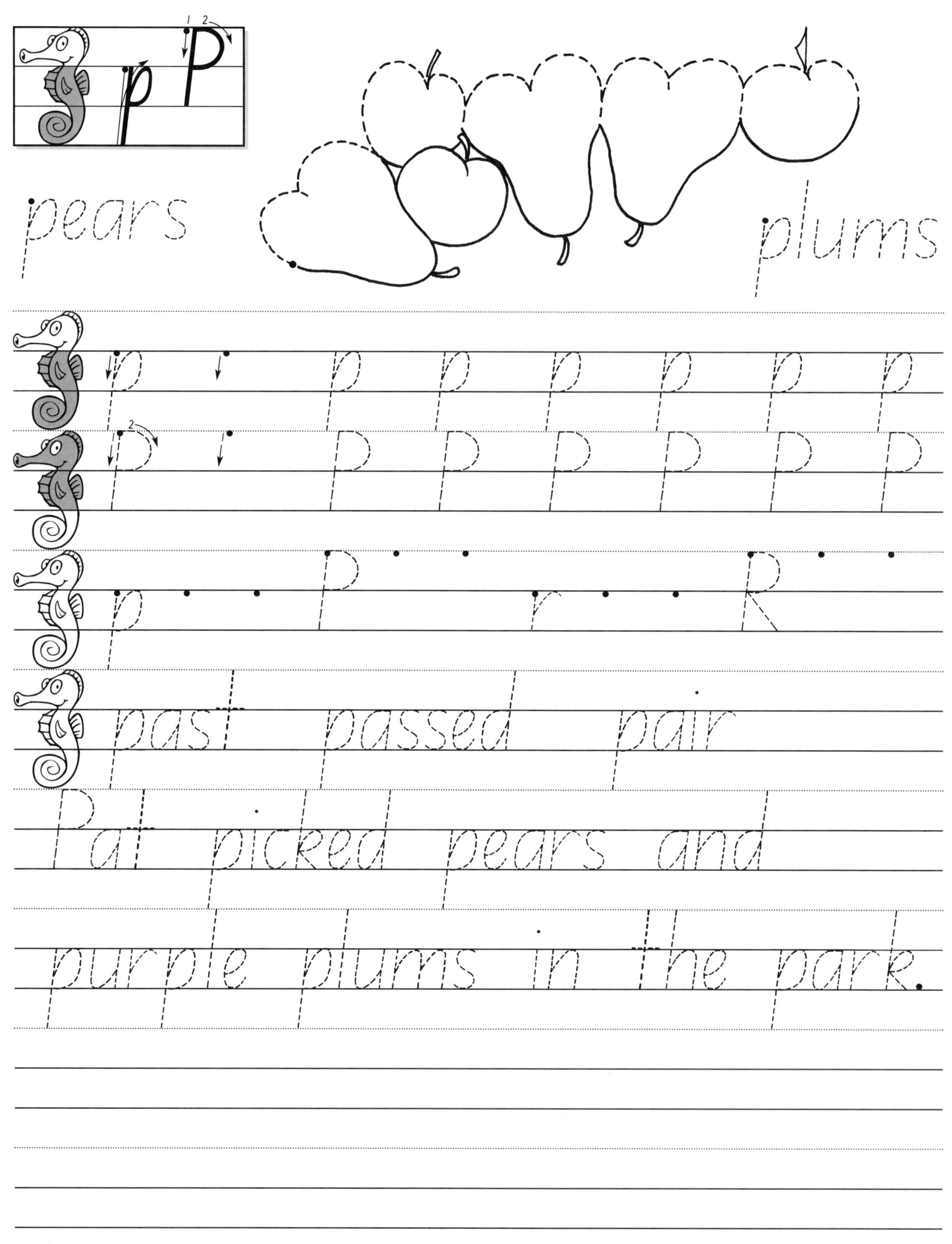

Re-trace all the p's in the sentence in purple. Circle your best p.

Write all the body and tail letters, three times each.

Trace. Fill in the p's. Re-write the words that contain the letter p.

Put a wavy line under the hopping pattern letters in the sentence.

✓ your best k.

Bas ing shar s eat plan ton.

Find **k** in these letters.

h b p r n m

wa_ ta_ sta_ cha_

Trace. Fill in the missing **k**'s. Copy.

sha_e lea_

wa_e lee_

ta_e wea_

sna_e wee_

ra_e _eep

Trace. Copy. Write the matching capital letter.

m n r

h b p k

Trace and copy.

keep heap

bump hump

rink brink

Mark the starting point in red. Trace, then copy.
Colour the seahorse to show where the letters sit in the lines.

m r n

h b k

Draw the seahorse. Write all the hopping pattern letters.

Trace the wave patterns to complete the pictures.

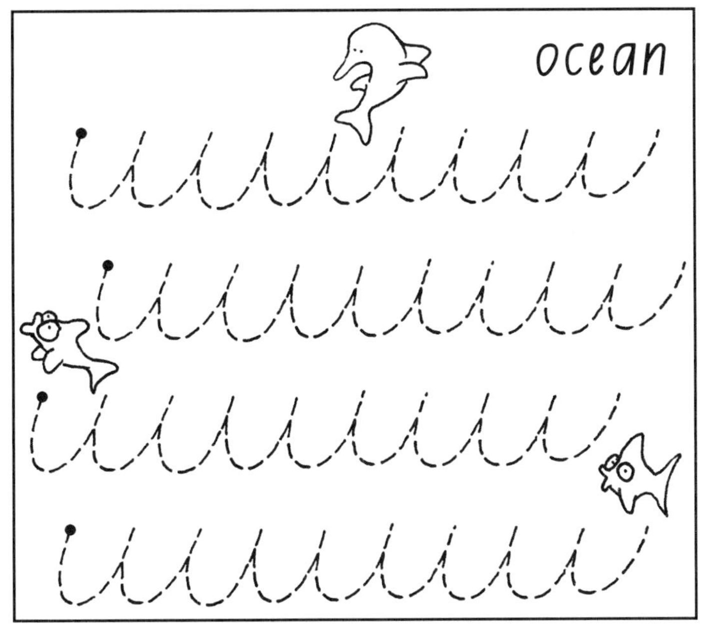

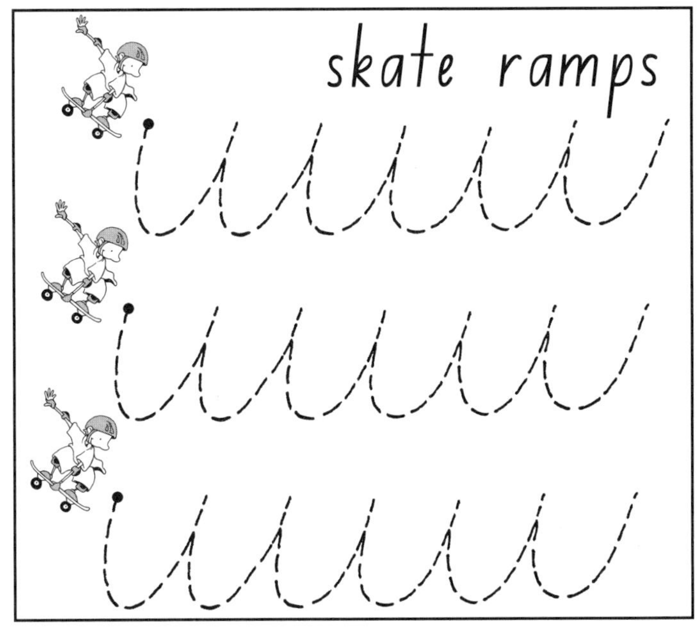

Colour the wedges in the wave pattern letters in the sentence.
Re-trace your best u in blue.

The s_rf is lo_d!

Trace the wave pattern letters.

u v r w n m a c o

fo_rteen 14 forty-fo_r 44

Trace. Fill in the missing **u**'s. Copy.

exc_se

cost_me

perf_me

vol_me

conf_se

Re-trace all the v's in the sentence in blue. Put a wavy line under your best v.

Observe the curvy vases.

Trace the body letters.

v y g u w c q a o d

se_enteen 17 se_enty 70

Trace. Fill in the missing v's. Copy.

tele_ision

cur_e

ri_er

sto_e

_olcano

Underline the wave pattern letters in the sentence.

✓ your best w.

hat a s arm of asps!

Trace. Copy. Colour the wedges.

w u a y g

t elve 12 inter

Add **w**. Trace. Copy. Circle the silent letter in each word.

hiff

hen

heel

hich

hiskers

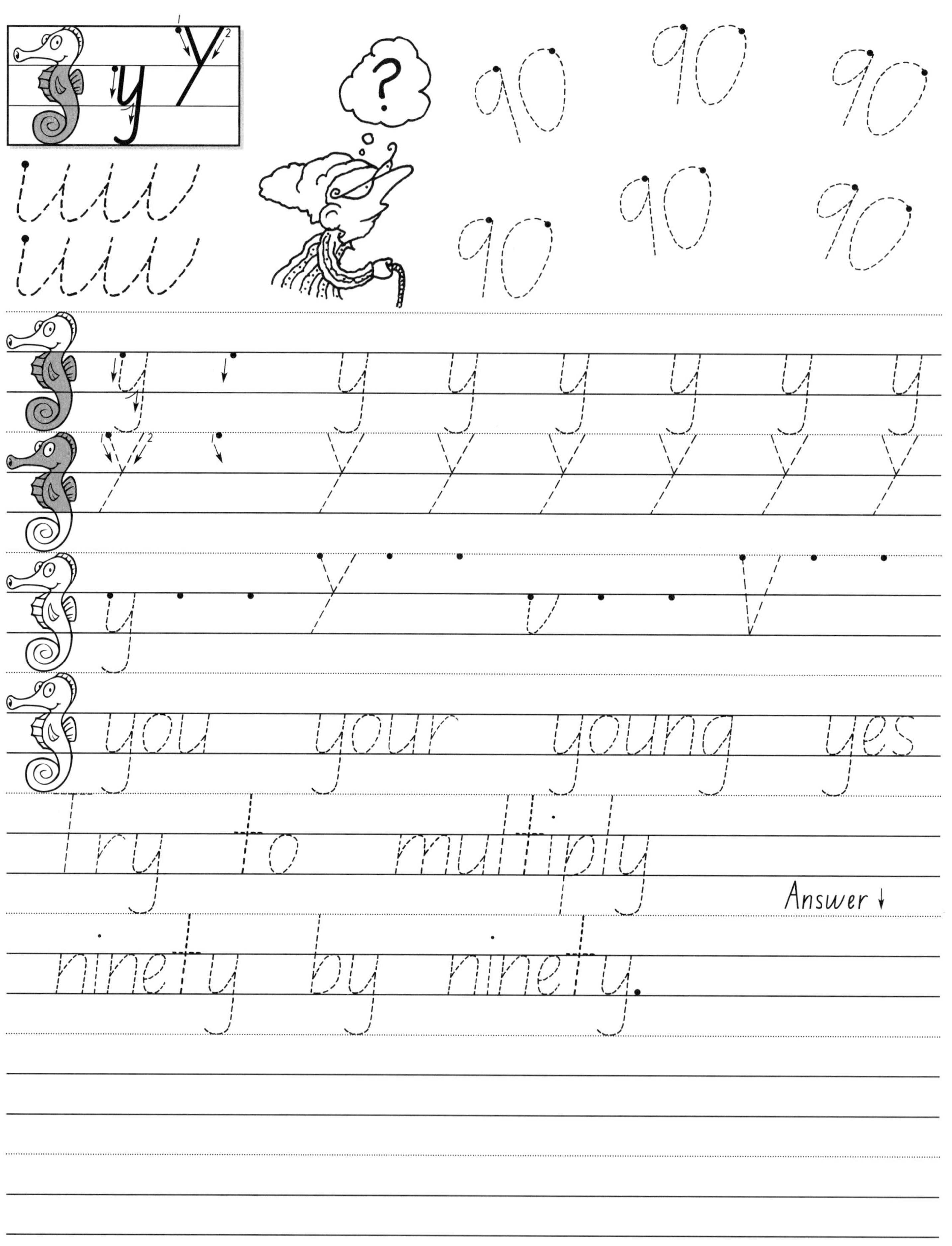

Look at the sentence. Colour the wedges in the wave pattern letters red. Circle your best y.

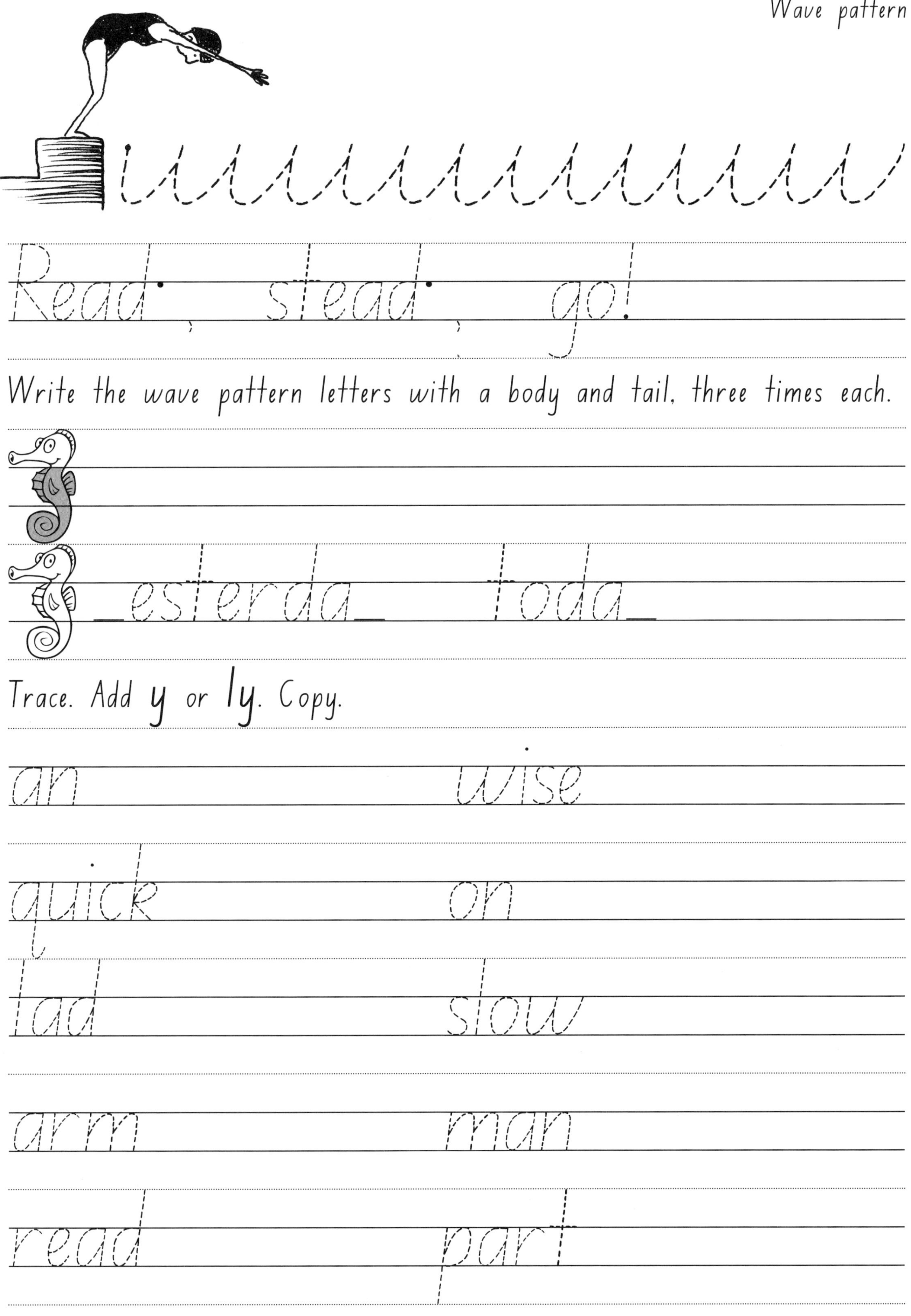

Read_, stead_, go!

Write the wave pattern letters with a body and tail, three times each.

esterda toda_

Trace. Add y or ly. Copy.

an wise

quick on

lad slow

arm man

read part

Underline the wave pattern letters in the sentence. Circle your best a.

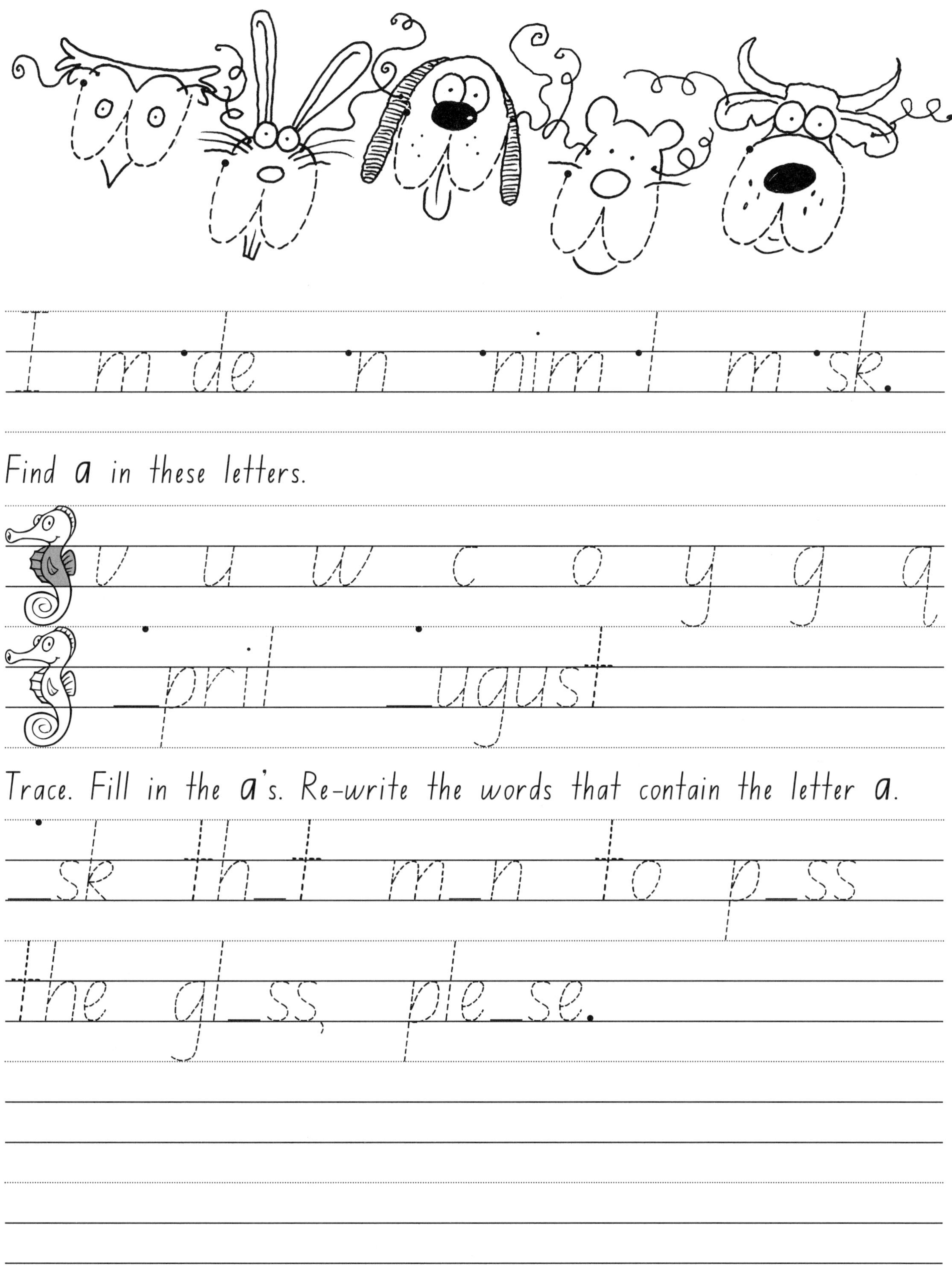

Find a in these letters.

Trace. Fill in the a's. Re-write the words that contain the letter a.

Circle the c's in the sentence. ✓your best c.

Wave pattern

caw caw caw caw caw caw

"_aw, _aw," _ried the _row.

Trace and copy these wave pattern letters.

c a o g e

_hristmas lun_h

Trace. Fill in the missing c's. Copy. Draw.

_heese

bran_h

_hi_ken

_ho_olate

pea_h

Underline the o's in the sentence. ✓ your best o.

D_ y_u like _ysters?

Find o in these letters.

c a e g q w u v

_d_ber t_m_rr_w

Add oo. Trace. Cross out the words that don't rhyme with book.

b__k c__k t__k

g__d h__k f__t

l__k n__k f__l

sh__k l__p t__th

g__se mist__k s__n

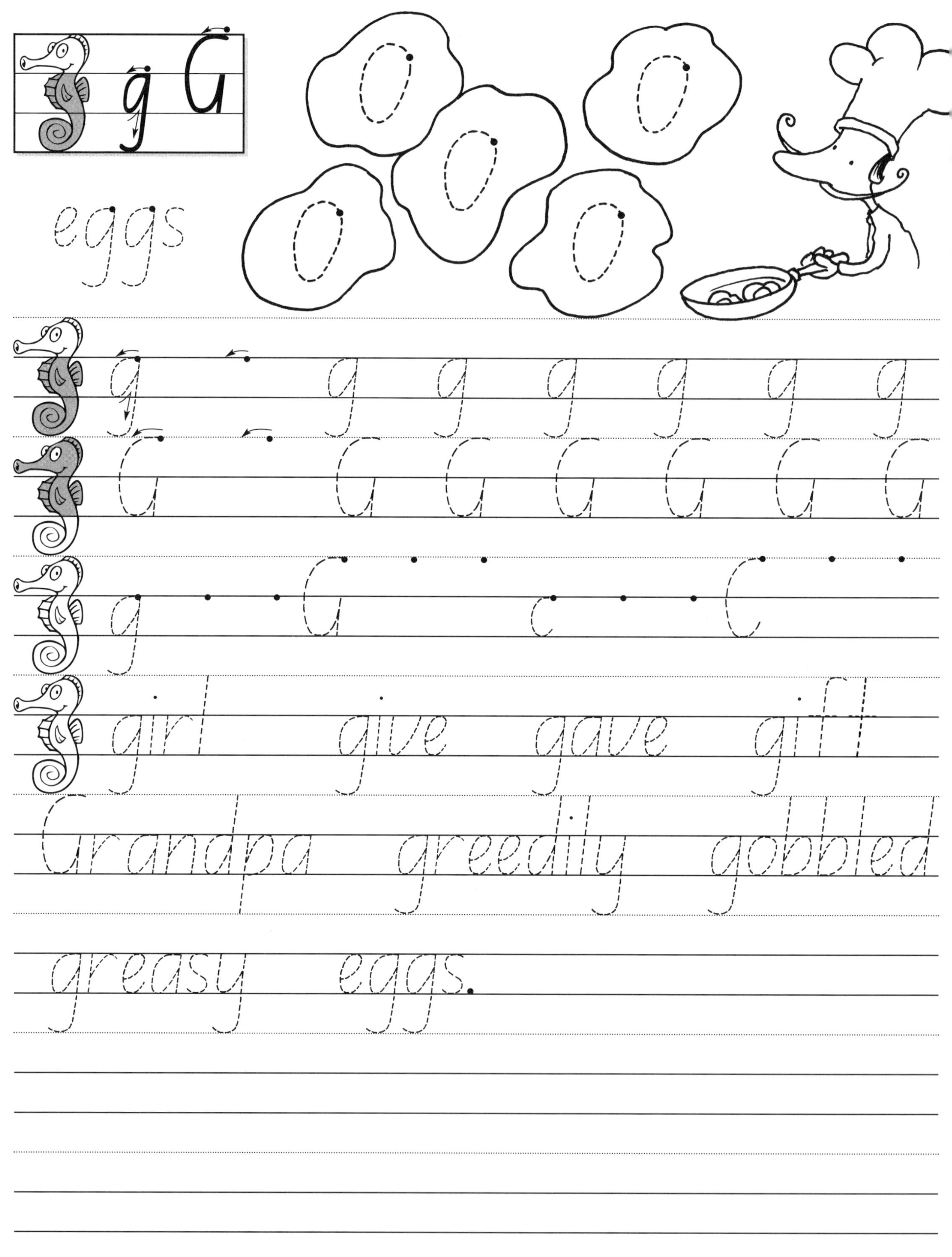

Look at the sentence. Colour the wedges in the wave pattern letters.
Circle your best g.

6
4
9
5
2
3
Ready? Set?
Trace. Colour the wedges. Copy.
g y q g
ei_hty 80 ei_hth 8th
Trace. Add g. Re-write the words that contain a soft g, as in giraffe.
a_e _low dan_er
_iant _in_er _rapes

Look at the sentence. Re-trace the letter that always comes after q.
Put a □ around your best q.

Who's yelling?

Wave pattern

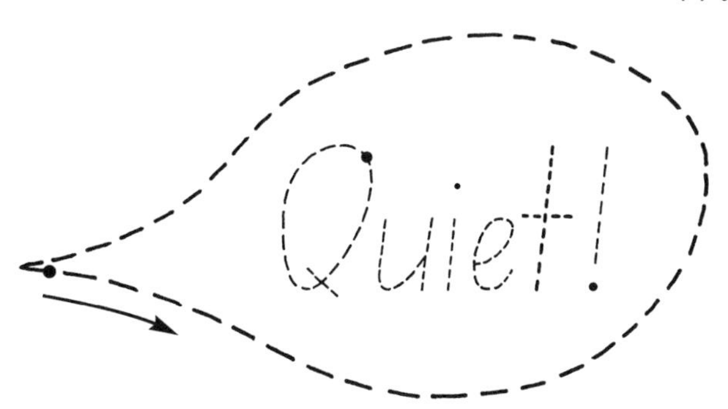

"__uiet!" yelled __________.

Trace the body and tail letters.

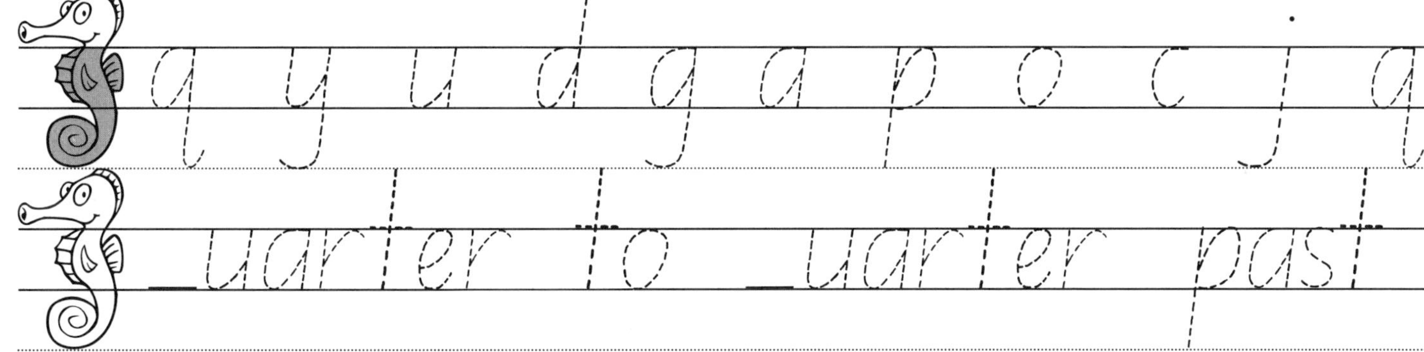

Add **qu**. Trace. Copy. Draw. For the last one, just trace then draw.

__een

s__are

s__id

__it

__estion mark

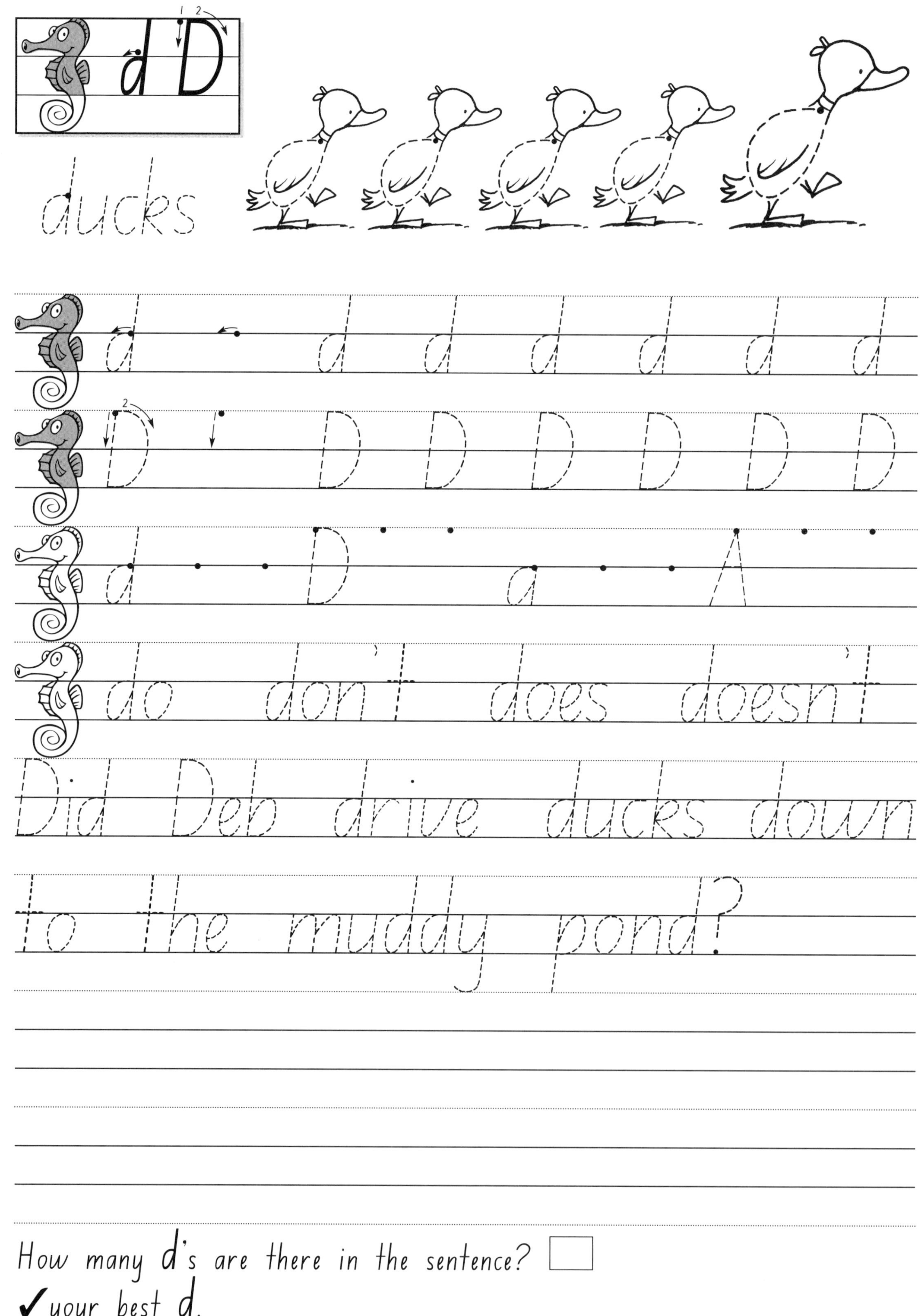

How many d's are there in the sentence?

✓ your best d.

Wave pattern

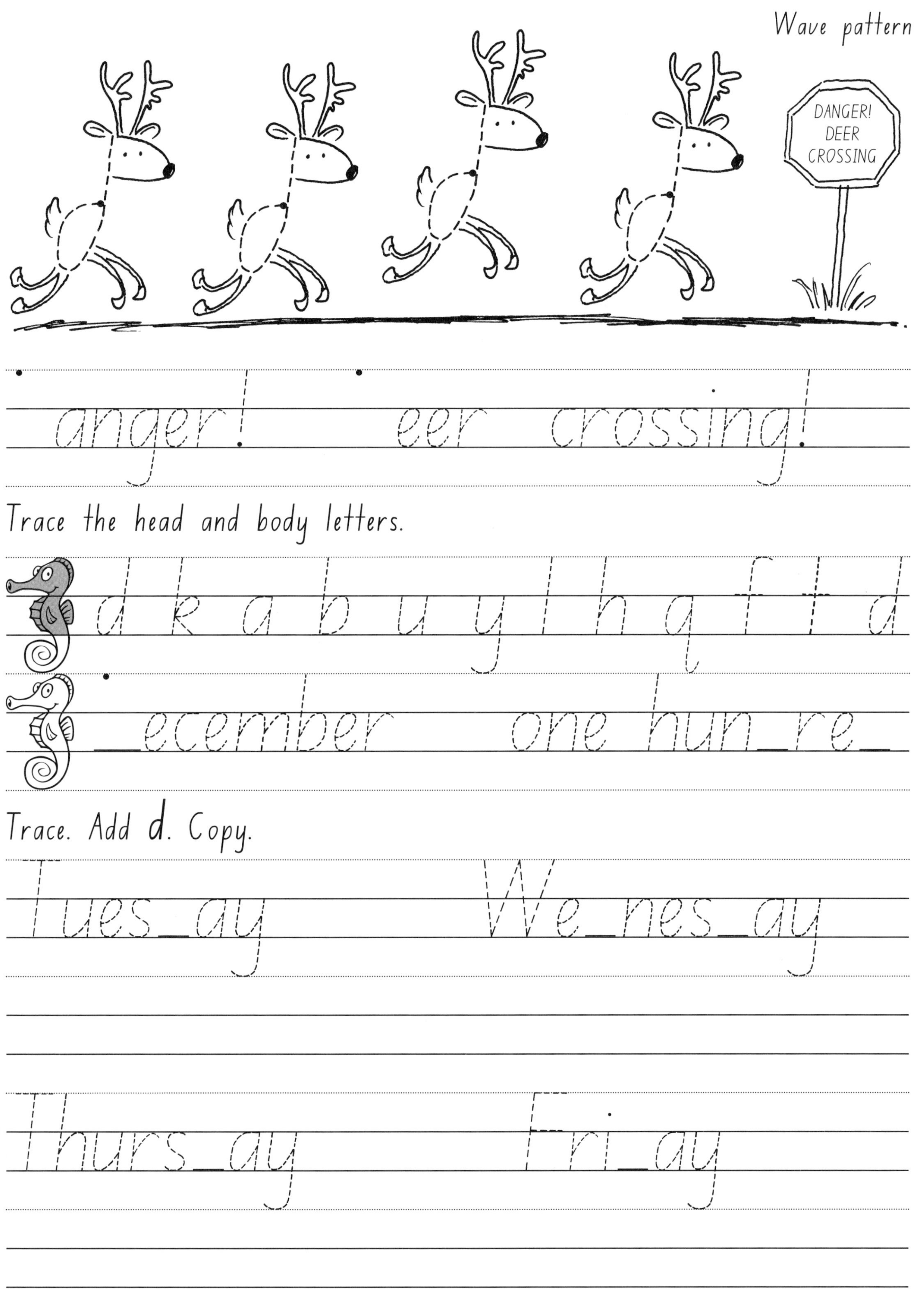

anger! eer crossing!

Trace the head and body letters.

d k a b u y l h q f t d

_ecember one hun_re_

Trace. Add d. Copy.

Tues_ay We_nes_ay

Thurs_ay Fri_ay

Re-trace the **e**'s in the sentence in red. Circle your best **e**.

Wave pattern

Draw some other green vegetables.

Gr..n p.as tast. sw..t.

Find **e** in these letters.

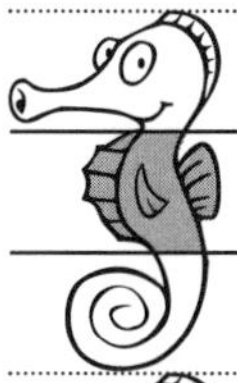

o a c d q y g v w u

_l_v_n l l __ast_r

Trace. Add **ee**. Cross out the words that don't rhyme with meet.

m__t sw__t sl__p

gr__n sh__t wh__l

str__t gr__t ch__k

f__t t__th sp__d

d__r f__l sh__t

Draw a squiggly line under your best s.

kateboarding i ________________.

Trace the body letters.

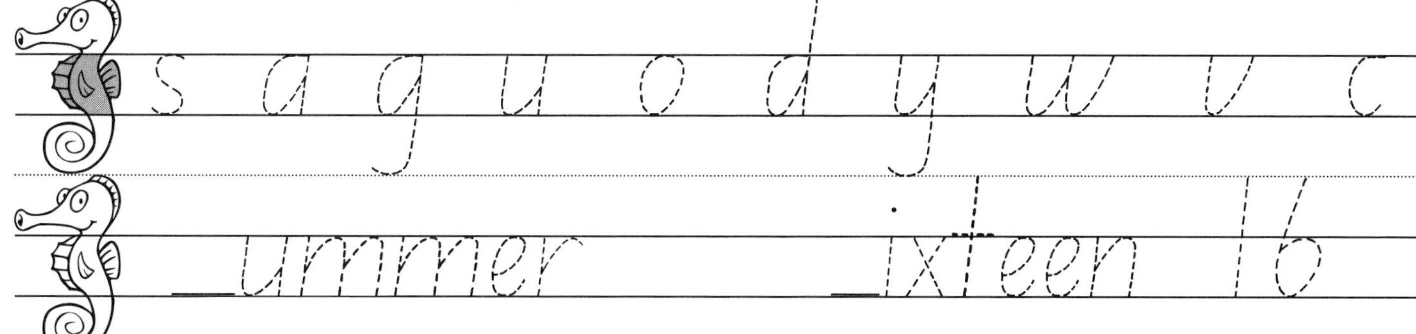

Trace. Fill in the missing s's. Re-write the words that contain ss.

Gue__ which que__!

cha_ed the po__um

acro__ the gra__.

Trace. Copy. Write the matching capital letter.

q w g o

u y a c

e d v s

Trace and copy.

quay cage

dove sew

Mark the starting point in green. Trace, then copy.
Colour the seahorse to show where the letters sit in the lines.

y g q

e o a

Draw the seahorse. Write all the wave pattern letters.

Trace. Copy.

40
40
0 10 20
1 11 30
2 12 40
3 13 50
4 14 60
5 15 70
6 16 80
7 17 90
8 18 100
9 19 1000

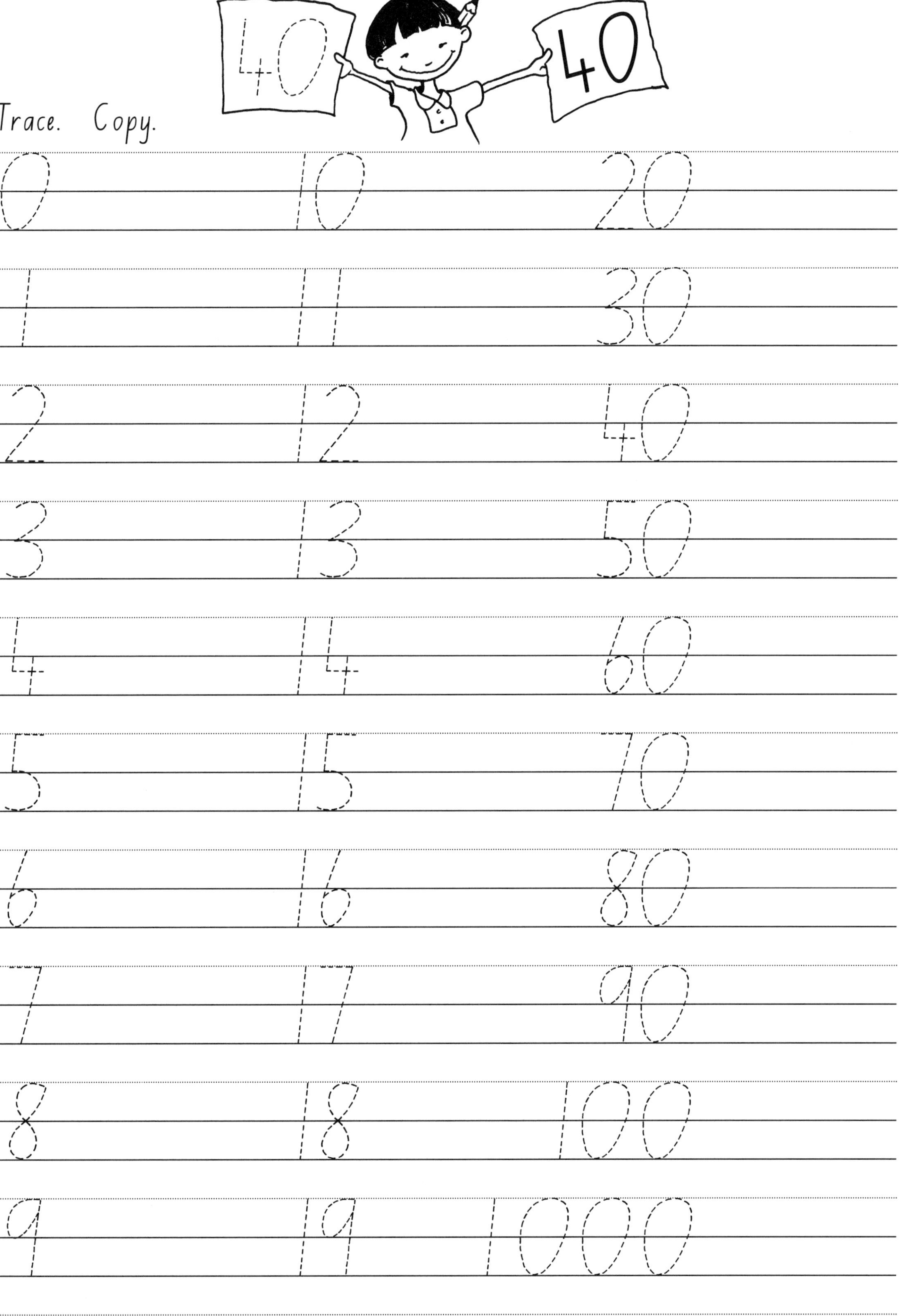

Trace. Copy.

1 one

2 two

3 three

4 four

5 five

6 six

7 seven

8 eight

9 nine

10 ten

Trace. Fill in the numerals that are missing.

1 2 4 6 7

9 10 12 13

15 17 18 20

Trace. Match the numeral to the number word.

12	ten	thirteen	16
17	eighteen	nineteen	14
18	eleven	fifteen	19
11	seventeen	sixteen	13
10	twelve	fourteen	15

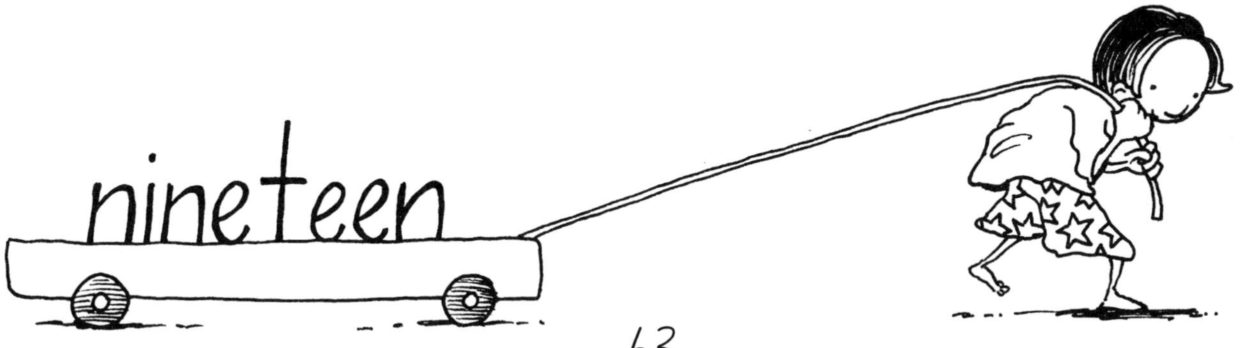

nineteen

Trace. Copy.
For the last one, just trace.

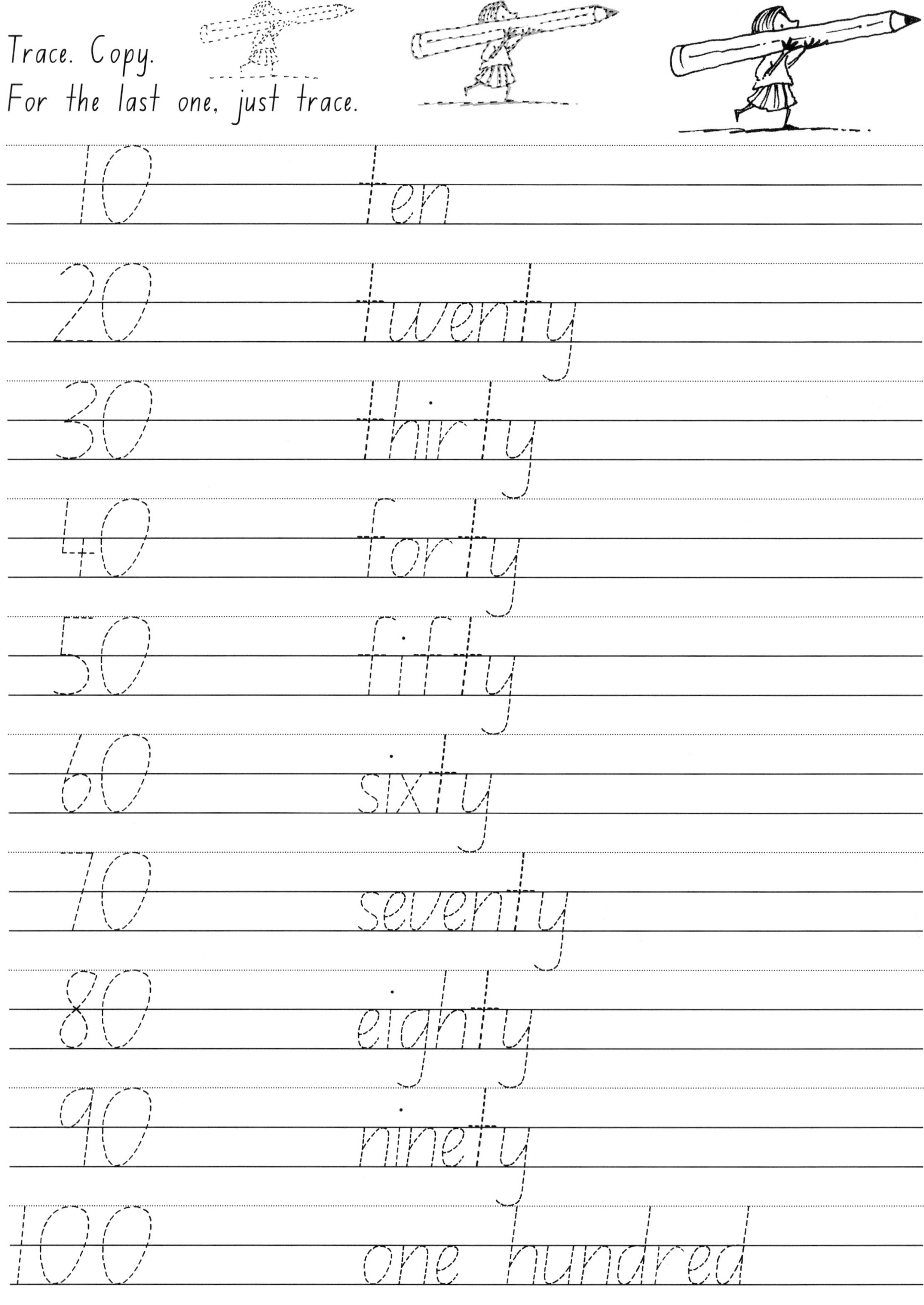